Easy -to- Bake

RECIPES

Publications International, Ltd.

Favorite Brand Name Recipes at www.fbnr.com

Some of the products listed in this publication may be in limited distribution.

Pictured on the front cover *(clockwise from top left):* Cinnamon Chip Filled Crescents *(page 56),* Apple-Raisin Cobbler Pie *(page 34),* Easy Egg Nog Pound Cake *(page 32)* and Chocolate Nut Bars *(page 16).*

Pictured on the back cover: Decadent Brownie Pie *(page 40).*

ISBN: 0-7853-8848-6

Manufactured in China.

8 7 6 5 4 3 2 1

Microwave Cooking: Microwave ovens vary in wattage. Use the cooking times as guidelines and check for doneness before adding more time.

Preparation/Cooking Times: Preparation times are based on the approximate amount of time required to assemble the recipe before cooking, baking, chilling or serving. These times include preparation steps such as measuring, chopping and mixing. The fact that some preparations and cooking can be done simultaneously is taken into account. Preparation of optional ingredients and serving suggestions is not included.

table of contents

Speedy Cookies 4

Express Bars 16

Quick Cakes 24

Effortless Pies 34

Simple Breads 48

Acknowledgments 62

Index 63

speedy cookies

Crispy's Irresistible Peanut Butter Marbles

Makes 5 dozen cookies

> **1 package (18 ounces) refrigerated peanut butter cookie dough**
> **2 cups "M&M's"® Milk Chocolate Mini Baking Bits, divided**
> **1 cup crisp rice cereal, divided (optional)**
> **1 package (18 ounces) refrigerated sugar cookie dough**
> **¼ cup unsweetened cocoa powder**

In large bowl combine peanut butter dough, 1 cup "M&M's"® Milk Chocolate Mini Baking Bits and ½ cup cereal, if desired. Remove dough to small bowl; set aside. In large bowl combine sugar dough and cocoa powder until well blended. Stir in remaining 1 cup "M&M's"® Milk Chocolate Mini Baking Bits and remaining ½ cup cereal, if desired. Remove half the dough to small bowl; set aside. Combine half the peanut butter dough with half the chocolate dough by folding together just enough to marble. Shape marbled dough into 8×2-inch log. Wrap log in plastic wrap. Repeat with remaining doughs. Refrigerate logs 2 hours. To bake, preheat oven to 350°F. Cut dough into ¼-inch-thick slices. Place about 2 inches apart on ungreased cookie sheets. Bake 12 to 14 minutes until just set. Cool 1 minute on cookie sheets; cool completely on wire racks. Store in tightly covered container.

Crispy's Irresistible Peanut Butter Marbles

Nutty Lemon Crescents

Makes about 4 dozen cookies

1 package (18 ounces) refrigerated sugar cookie dough
1 cup chopped pecans, toasted*
1 tablespoon grated lemon peel
1½ cups powdered sugar, divided

*To toast pecans, spread in single layer on baking sheet. Bake in preheated 350°F oven 8 to 10 minutes or until golden brown, stirring frequently.

Preheat oven to 375°F. Remove dough from wrapper according to package directions.

Combine dough, pecans and lemon peel in large bowl. Stir until thoroughly blended. Shape level tablespoonfuls of dough into crescent shapes. Place 2 inches apart on ungreased cookie sheets. Bake 8 to 9 minutes or until set and very lightly browned. Cool 2 minutes on cookie sheets. Remove to wire racks.

Place 1 cup powdered sugar in shallow bowl. Roll warm cookies in powdered sugar. Cool completely. Sift remaining ½ cup powdered sugar over cookies just before serving.

3-Minute No-Bake Cookies

Makes about 3 dozen cookies

2 cups granulated sugar
½ cup (1 stick) margarine or butter
½ cup 2% milk
⅓ cup unsweetened cocoa powder
3 cups QUAKER® Oats (quick or old fashioned, uncooked)

In large saucepan, combine sugar, margarine, milk and cocoa. Bring to boil over medium heat, stirring frequently. Continue boiling 3 minutes. Remove from heat. Stir in oats; mix well. Quickly drop by tablespoonfuls onto waxed paper or greased cookie sheet. Let stand until set. Store tightly covered at room temperature.

Nutty Lemon Crescents

Orange Pecan Cookies

Makes about 3 dozen cookies

1 package (about 17 ounces) sugar cookie mix
½ cup butter, melted
1 egg, slightly beaten
1 teaspoon grated orange peel
½ cup chopped pecans
½ cup powdered sugar
1½ teaspoons orange juice

Preheat oven to 375°F.

Combine cookie mix, butter, egg and orange peel in large bowl. Stir with spoon until well blended. Stir in pecans.

Drop dough by rounded teaspoonfuls onto *ungreased* cookie sheets about 2 inches apart. Bake for 7 to 8 minutes or until set. Cool 1 minute on cookie sheets. Remove to wire racks; cool completely.

Combine powdered sugar and orange juice in small bowl; stir until well blended. Drizzle over top of cooled cookies. Allow glaze to set before storing between layers of waxed paper in airtight container.

Chips Ahoy!® Wiches

Makes 12 sandwich cookies

24 CHIPS AHOY!® Chocolate Chip Cookies
3 cups any flavor ice cream, sherbet, frozen yogurt or whipped topping
Sprinkles, chocolate chips, chopped nuts, toasted or tinted coconut, or other assorted small candies

1. Spread ¼ cup ice cream on flat side of each of 12 cookies. Place remaining cookies on top. Roll or lightly press edges in sprinkles.

2. Freeze until firm, about 4 hours.

Peanut Butter Chipwiches: Spread about 1 tablespoon peanut butter on flat side of each of 12 cookies; top with a banana slice. Continue as directed above.

Orange Pecan Cookies

Flourless Peanut Butter Cookies

Makes about 2 dozen cookies

1 cup peanut butter
1 cup packed light brown sugar
1 egg
**24 milk chocolate candy stars or other solid milk chocolate
candy**

Preheat oven to 350°F. Combine peanut butter, sugar and egg in medium bowl; beat until blended and smooth.

Shape dough into 24 balls about 1½ inches in diameter. Place 2 inches apart on ungreased cookie sheets. Press one chocolate star on top of each cookie. Bake 10 to 12 minutes or until set. Transfer to wire racks to cool completely.

Coconut Clouds

Makes 3½ dozen cookies

2⅔ cups flaked coconut, divided
**1 package DUNCAN HINES® Moist Deluxe® Classic Yellow
Cake Mix**
1 egg
½ cup vegetable oil
¼ cup water
1 teaspoon almond extract

1. Preheat oven to 350°F. Reserve 1⅓ cups coconut in medium bowl.

2. Combine cake mix, egg, oil, water and almond extract in large bowl. Beat at low speed with electric mixer. Stir in remaining 1⅓ cups coconut. Drop rounded teaspoonful dough into reserved coconut. Roll to cover lightly. Place on ungreased baking sheet. Repeat with remaining dough, placing balls 2 inches apart. Bake at 350°F 10 to 12 minutes or until light golden brown. Cool 1 minute on baking sheets. Remove to cooling racks. Cool completely. Store in airtight container.

Cook's Note: To save time when forming dough into balls, use a 1-inch spring-operated cookie scoop. Spring-operated cookie scoops are available at kitchen specialty shops.

Flourless Peanut Butter Cookies

speedycookies

Easy Lemon Cookies

Makes 4 dozen cookies

1 package DUNCAN HINES® Moist Deluxe® Lemon Cake Mix
2 eggs
½ cup vegetable oil
1 teaspoon grated lemon peel
Pecan halves, for garnish

1. Preheat oven to 350°F.

2. Combine cake mix, eggs, oil and lemon peel in large bowl. Stir until thoroughly blended. Drop by rounded teaspoonfuls 2 inches apart onto ungreased cookie sheets. Press pecan half in center of each cookie. Bake at 350°F for 9 to 11 minutes or until edges are light golden brown. Cool 1 minute on cookie sheets. Remove to wire racks. Cool completely. Store in airtight container.

Tip: You may substitute whole almonds or walnut halves for the pecan halves.

Chocolate Chip 'n Oatmeal Cookies

Makes about 4 dozen cookies

1 package (18.25 or 18.5 ounces) yellow cake mix
1 cup quick-cooking rolled oats, uncooked
¾ cup butter or margarine, softened
2 eggs
1 cup HERSHEY'S Semi-Sweet Chocolate Chips

Heat oven to 350°F.

Combine cake mix, oats, butter and eggs in large bowl; mix well. Stir in chocolate chips. Drop by rounded teaspoons onto ungreased cookie sheets.

Bake 10 to 12 minutes or until very lightly browned. Cool slightly; remove from cookie sheets to wire racks. Cool completely.

Easy Lemon Cookies

speedycookies

Chocolate Peanut Butter Chip Cookies

Makes about 4 dozen cookies

Prep Time: 15 minutes
Bake Time: 6 to 8 minutes

- 8 (1-ounce) squares semi-sweet chocolate
- 3 tablespoons butter or margarine
- 1 (14-ounce) can EAGLE® BRAND Sweetened Condensed Milk (NOT evaporated milk)
- 2 cups biscuit baking mix
- 1 egg
- 1 teaspoon vanilla extract
- 1 cup (6 ounces) peanut butter-flavored chips

1. Preheat oven to 350°F. In large saucepan, over low heat, melt chocolate and butter with Eagle Brand; remove from heat. Add biscuit mix, egg and vanilla; with mixer, beat until smooth and well blended.

2. Let mixture cool to room temperature. Stir in peanut butter chips. Shape into 1¼-inch balls. Place 2 inches apart on ungreased baking sheets. Bake 6 to 8 minutes or until tops are slightly crusty. Cool. Store tightly covered at room temperature.

Chocolate Macadamia Chippers

Makes 2 dozen cookies

- 1 package (18 ounces) refrigerated chocolate chip cookie dough
- 3 tablespoons unsweetened cocoa powder
- ½ cup coarsely chopped macadamia nuts

Preheat oven to 375°F. Remove dough from wrapper according to package directions.

Place dough in medium bowl; stir in cocoa until well blended. (Dough may be kneaded lightly, if desired.) Stir in nuts. Drop by heaping tablespoons 2 inches apart onto ungreased cookie sheets.

Bake 9 to 11 minutes or until almost set. Transfer to wire racks to cool completely.

14

Chocolate Peanut Butter Chip Cookies

express bars

Chocolate Nut Bars

Makes 24 to 36 bars

Prep Time: 10 minutes
Bake Time: 33 to 38 minutes

> 1¾ cups graham cracker crumbs
> ½ cup (1 stick) butter or margarine, melted
> 1 (14-ounce) can EAGLE® BRAND Sweetened Condensed Milk (NOT evaporated milk)
> 2 cups (12 ounces) semi-sweet chocolate chips, divided
> 1 teaspoon vanilla extract
> 1 cup chopped nuts

1. Preheat oven to 375°F. Combine crumbs and butter; press firmly on bottom of 13×9-inch baking pan. Bake 8 minutes. *Reduce oven temperature to 350°F.*

2. In small saucepan, melt Eagle Brand with 1 cup chocolate chips and vanilla. Spread chocolate mixture over prepared crust. Top with remaining 1 cup chocolate chips, then nuts; press down firmly.

3. Bake 25 to 30 minutes. Cool. Chill if desired. Cut into bars. Store loosely covered at room temperature.

Chocolate Nut Bars

expressbars

Easy Turtle Squares

Makes 24 bar cookies

    1 package (about 18 ounces) chocolate cake mix
½ cup butter, melted
¼ cup milk
    1 cup (6-ounce package) semisweet chocolate chips
    1 cup chopped pecans, divided
    1 jar (12 ounces) caramel ice cream topping

Preheat oven to 350°F. Spray 13×9-inch pan with nonstick cooking spray.

Combine cake mix, butter and milk in large bowl. Press half of the cake mixture into prepared baking pan.

Bake 7 to 8 minutes or until batter begins to form crust. Carefully remove from oven. Sprinkle chocolate chips and ½ cup pecans over partially baked crust. Drizzle caramel topping over chips and pecans. Drop spoonfuls of remaining cake batter over caramel mixture; sprinkle with remaining ½ cup pecans.

Return to oven; bake 18 to 20 minutes longer or until top of cake layer springs back when lightly touched. (Caramel center will be soft.) Cool completely on wire rack. Cut into squares.

Easy Turtle Squares

Coconut Raspberry Bars

Makes approximately 3 to 3½ dozen bars

2 cups graham cracker crumbs
½ cup butter, melted
1⅓ cups (3½-ounce can) flaked coconut
1 can (14 ounces) sweetened condensed milk
1 cup red raspberry jam or preserves
½ cup chopped pecans
½ cup semisweet chocolate chips
½ cup white chocolate chips

Preheat oven to 350°F.

Combine graham cracker crumbs and butter in medium bowl. Press on bottom of *ungreased* 13×9-inch baking pan to make crust. Sprinkle with coconut; pour sweetened condensed milk evenly over coconut.

Bake 20 to 25 minutes or until lightly browned; cool completely in pan on wire rack.

Spread jam over coconut layer; sprinkle with pecans. Chill for 3 to 4 hours.

Place semisweet chocolate chips in small resealable plastic bag; seal bag. Microwave at HIGH (100%) 1 minute. Turn bag over; heat at HIGH 1 to 2 minutes or until chocolate is melted. Knead bag until chocolate is smooth. Cut off very tiny corner of bag; drizzle chocolate onto jam layer. Melt white chocolate chips as directed for chocolate chips. Drizzle over top of chocolate layer to make lacy effect; chill until chocolate is set. Cut into bars.

Coconut Raspberry Bars

Creamy Lemon Bars

Makes 2 dozen bars

Prep Time: 15 minutes
Bake Time: 35 minutes

> 1 package (2-layer size) lemon cake mix
> 3 large eggs
> ½ cup oil
> 2 packages (8 ounces each) PHILADELPHIA® Cream Cheese, softened
> 1 container (8 ounces) BREAKSTONE'S® or KNUDSEN® Sour Cream
> ½ cup granulated sugar
> 1 teaspoon grated lemon peel
> 1 tablespoon lemon juice
> Powdered sugar

MIX cake mix, 1 egg and oil. Press mixture onto bottom and up sides of lightly greased 15×10×1-inch baking pan. Bake at 350°F for 10 minutes.

BEAT cream cheese with electric mixer on medium speed until smooth. Add remaining 2 eggs, sour cream, granulated sugar, peel and juice; mix until blended. Pour batter into crust.

BAKE at 350°F for 30 to 35 minutes or until filling is just set in center and edges are light golden brown. Cool. Sprinkle with powdered sugar. Cut into bars. Store leftover bars in refrigerator.

Creamy Lemon Bars

quick
cakes

Easy Cappuccino Cake

Makes 14 servings

Prep Time: 25 minutes

- **1 package (2-layer size) white cake mix**
- **4 tablespoons MAXWELL HOUSE® Instant Coffee, divided**
- **¼ cup milk plus 1 tablespoon milk**
- **4 squares BAKER'S® Semi-Sweet Baking Chocolate, melted**
- **2 tubs (8 ounces each) COOL WHIP® Whipped Topping, thawed, divided**

HEAT oven to 350°F.

PREPARE and bake cake mix as directed on package for 8- or 9-inch round pans, adding 2 tablespoons instant coffee to cake mix.

POUR ¼ cup milk and 1 tablespoon instant coffee into small bowl, stirring until coffee is dissolved. Slowly stir into melted chocolate until smooth. Cool completely. Gently stir in 1 tub of whipped topping. Refrigerate 20 minutes or until well chilled.

MEANWHILE, mix 1 tablespoon milk and 1 tablespoon coffee until dissolved. Gently stir into remaining tub of whipped topping.

COVER one cake layer with chocolate mixture. Place second cake layer on top. Frost top and side of cake with coffee-flavored whipped topping. Refrigerate until ready to serve.

Variation: If desired, omit the coffee for a delicious plain chocolate filled layer cake.

Easy Cappuccino Cake

quickcakes

Luscious Lemon Poke Cake

Makes 12 servings

Preparation Time: 30 minutes
Refrigerating Time: 4 hours

> **2 baked 8- or 9-inch round white cake layers, cooled completely**
> **2 cups boiling water**
> **1 package (8-serving size) *or* 2 packages (4-serving size) JELL-O® Brand Lemon Flavor Gelatin Dessert**
> **1 tub (8 or 12 ounces) COOL WHIP® Whipped Topping, thawed**

PLACE cake layers, top sides up, in 2 clean 8- or 9-inch round cake pans. Pierce cake with large fork at ½-inch intervals.

STIR boiling water into gelatin in medium bowl at least 2 minutes until completely dissolved. Carefully pour 1 cup of the gelatin over 1 cake layer. Pour remaining gelatin over second cake layer. Refrigerate 3 hours.

DIP 1 cake pan in warm water 10 seconds; unmold onto serving plate. Spread with about 1 cup of the whipped topping. Unmold second cake layer; carefully place on first cake layer. Frost top and side of cake with remaining whipped topping.

REFRIGERATE at least 1 hour or until ready to serve. Decorate as desired.

Luscious Lemon Poke Cake

quickcakes

Chocolate Toffee Crunch Fantasy

Makes 12 servings

1 package DUNCAN HINES® Moist Deluxe® Devil's Food Cake Mix
12 bars (1.4 ounces each) chocolate covered toffee bars, divided
3 cups whipping cream, chilled

1. Preheat oven to 350°F. Grease and flour 10-inch tube pan.

2. Prepare, bake and cool cake following package directions. Split cake horizontally into three layers; set aside. Chop 11 candy bars into pea-size pieces (see Tip). Whip cream until stiff peaks form. Fold candy pieces into whipped cream.

3. To assemble, place one split cake layer on serving plate. Spread 1½ cups whipped cream mixture on top. Repeat with remaining layers and whipped cream mixture. Frost sides and top with remaining filling. Chop remaining candy bar coarsely. Sprinkle over top. Refrigerate until ready to serve.

Tip: To quickly chop toffee candy bars, place a few bars in food processor fitted with steel blade. Pulse several times until pea-size pieces form. Repeat with remaining candy bars.

Chocolate Toffee Crunch Fantasy

Banana Split Cupcakes

Makes 30 cupcakes

> 1 (18¼ ounces) yellow cake mix, divided
> 1 cup water
> 1 cup mashed ripe bananas
> 3 eggs
> 1 cup chopped drained maraschino cherries
> 1½ cups miniature semisweet chocolate chips, divided
> 1½ cups prepared vanilla frosting
> 1 cup marshmallow creme
> 1 teaspoon shortening
> 30 whole maraschino cherries, drained and patted dry

Preheat oven to 350°F. Line 30 regular-size (2½-inch) muffin cups with paper muffin cup liners.

Reserve 2 tablespoons cake mix. Combine remaining cake mix, water, bananas and eggs in large bowl. Beat at low speed of electric mixer until moistened, about 30 seconds. Beat at medium speed 2 minutes. Combine chopped cherries and reserved cake mix in small bowl. Stir chopped cherry mixture and 1 cup chocolate chips into batter.

Spoon batter into prepared muffin cups. Bake 15 to 20 minutes or until toothpick inserted in centers comes out clean. Cool in pans on wire racks 10 minutes. Remove to wire racks; cool completely.

Combine frosting and marshmallow creme in medium bowl until well blended. Frost each cupcake with frosting mixture.

Combine remaining ½ cup chocolate chips and shortening in small microwavable bowl. Microwave at HIGH 30 to 45 seconds, stirring after 30 seconds, or until smooth. Drizzle chocolate mixture over cupcakes. Place one whole cherry on each cupcake.

Note: If desired, omit chocolate drizzle and top cupcakes with colored sprinkles.

Banana Split Cupcakes

quickcakes

Easy Egg Nog Pound Cake

Makes 1 (10-inch) cake

Prep Time: 10 minutes
Bake Time: 40 to 45 minutes

    1 (18.25-ounce) package yellow cake mix
    1 (4-serving-size) package instant vanilla pudding and pie
       filling mix
    ¾ cup **BORDEN**® Egg Nog
    ¾ cup vegetable oil
    4 eggs
    ½ teaspoon ground nutmeg
      Powdered sugar, if desired

1. Preheat oven to 350°F.

2. In large mixing bowl, combine cake mix, pudding mix, Borden Egg Nog and oil; beat at low speed until moistened. Add eggs and nutmeg; beat at medium-high speed 4 minutes.

3. Pour into greased and floured 10-inch fluted or tube pan.

4. Bake 40 to 45 minutes or until toothpick inserted near center comes out clean.

5. Cool 10 minutes; remove from pan. Cool completely. Sprinkle with powdered sugar, if desired.

Easy Egg Nog Pound Cake

effortless pies

Apple-Raisin Cobbler Pie

Makes 8 servings

Prep Time: 10 minutes
Baking Time: 35 minutes

- 2 (20-ounce) cans apple pie filling
- 1 cup raisins
- ¼ teaspoon ground nutmeg
- 1 (6-ounce) READY CRUST® Shortbread Pie Crust
- ⅓ cup all-purpose flour
- ¼ cup packed brown sugar
- 3 tablespoons butter or margarine, melted
- ¾ cup chopped walnuts

Preheat oven to 375°F.

Combine pie filling, raisins and nutmeg in large bowl. Spoon into crust. Combine flour and sugar in small bowl; stir in butter until crumbly. Stir in walnuts; sprinkle over filling.

Bake 35 to 45 minutes or until topping is golden.

Apple-Raisin Cobbler Pie

Confetti Pie

Makes 8 servings

Prep Time: 15 minutes plus refrigerating

>   **1 boiling water**
>   **1 package (4-serving size) JELL-O® Brand Lemon Flavor Gelatin**
>   **½ cup cold water**
>   **1 cup boiling water**
>   **1 package (4-serving size) JELL-O® Brand Orange Flavor Gelatin**
>   **½ cup cold orange juice**
>   **2 cups thawed COOL WHIP® Whipped Topping**
>   **⅓ cup multi-colored sprinkles**
>   **1 HONEY MAID® Honey Graham Pie Crust (9 inch)**

STIR 1 cup boiling water into lemon gelatin in medium bowl at least 2 minutes until completely dissolved. Stir in cold water. Pour into 8-inch square pan. Refrigerate 4 hours or until firm. Cut into ½-inch cubes.

STIR 1 cup boiling water into orange gelatin in large bowl at least 2 minutes until completely dissolved. Stir in orange juice. Refrigerate about 20 minutes or until slightly thickened (consistency of unbeaten egg whites). Gently stir in whipped topping. Gently stir in gelatin cubes and sprinkles. Refrigerate until mixture will mound. Pour into crust.

REFRIGERATE at least 4 hours or until firm. Garnish with additional whipped topping and sprinkles, if desired.

Great Substitutes: Try Berry Blue or Lime Flavor Gelatin instead of Lemon Flavor when making the gelatin cubes.

Confetti Pie

Pumpkin Pie Crunch

Makes 16 to 20 servings

> **1 can (16 ounces) solid pack pumpkin**
> **1 can (12 ounces) evaporated milk**
> **3 eggs**
> **1½ cups sugar**
> **4 teaspoons pumpkin pie spice**
> **½ teaspoon salt**
> **1 package DUNCAN HINES® Moist Deluxe® Classic Yellow Cake Mix**
> **1 cup chopped pecans**
> **1 cup butter or margarine, melted**
> **Whipped topping**

1. Preheat oven to 350°F. Grease bottom of 13×9×2-inch pan.

2. Combine pumpkin, evaporated milk, eggs, sugar, pumpkin pie spice and salt in large bowl. Pour into pan. Sprinkle dry cake mix evenly over pumpkin mixture. Top with pecans. Drizzle with melted butter. Bake at 350°F 50 to 55 minutes or until golden. Cool completely. Serve with whipped topping. Refrigerate leftovers.

Tip: For a richer flavor, try using Duncan Hines® Moist Deluxe® Butter Recipe Golden Cake Mix.

Pumpkin Pie Crunch

Decadent Brownie Pie

Makes 1 (9-inch) pie

Prep Time: 25 minutes
Bake Time: 45 to 50 minutes

    1 (9-inch) unbaked pastry shell
    1 cup (6 ounces) semi-sweet chocolate chips
    ¼ cup (½ stick) butter or margarine
    1 (14-ounce) can EAGLE® BRAND Sweetened Condensed
        Milk (NOT evaporated milk)
    ½ cup biscuit baking mix
    2 eggs
    1 teaspoon vanilla extract
    1 cup chopped nuts
      Vanilla ice cream

1. Preheat oven to 375°F. Bake pastry shell 10 minutes; remove from oven. Reduce oven temperature to 325°F.

2. In saucepan over low heat, melt chips with butter.

3. In mixing bowl, beat chocolate mixture with Eagle Brand, biscuit mix, eggs and vanilla until smooth. Add nuts. Pour into pastry shell.

4. Bake 35 to 40 minutes or until center is set. Serve warm or at room temperature with ice cream. Refrigerate leftovers.

Decadent Brownie Pie

Caramel-Pecan Pie

Makes 6 to 8 servings

3 eggs
⅔ cup sugar
1 cup (12-ounce jar) SMUCKER'S® Caramel Topping
¼ cup butter or margarine, melted
1½ cups pecan halves
1 (9-inch) unbaked pie shell

In mixing bowl, beat eggs slightly with fork. Add sugar, stirring until dissolved. Stir in topping and butter; mix well. Stir in pecan halves. Pour filling into pie shell.

Bake at 350°F for 45 minutes or until knife inserted near center comes out clean. Cool thoroughly on rack before serving. Cover and store in refrigerator.

Chocolate Peanut Butter Pie

Makes 8 servings

Prep Time: 5 minutes
Freezing Time: 6 hours

1 (14-ounce) can chocolate sweetened condensed milk
¼ cup creamy peanut butter
1 (8-ounce) tub frozen non-dairy whipped topping, thawed
1 (6-ounce) READY CRUST® Graham Cracker Pie Crust

Combine sweetened condensed milk and peanut butter in large bowl; mix well. Fold in whipped topping. Spoon into crust.

Freeze 6 hours. Garnish as desired. Freeze leftovers.

Caramel-Pecan Pie

White Chocolate Cranberry Tart

Makes 8 servings

1 refrigerated pie crust (half of 15-ounce package)
1 cup sugar
2 eggs
¼ cup butter, melted
2 teaspoons vanilla
½ cup all-purpose flour
1 package (6 ounces) white chocolate baking bar, chopped
½ cup chopped macadamia nuts, lightly toasted*
½ cup dried cranberries, coarsely chopped

Toast chopped macadamia nuts in hot skillet about 3 minutes or until fragrant.

Preheat oven to 350°F. Line 9-inch tart pan with removable bottom or pie pan with pie crust (refrigerate or freeze other crust for another use).

Combine sugar, eggs, butter and vanilla in large bowl; mix well. Stir in flour until well blended. Add white chocolate, nuts and cranberries.

Pour filling into unbaked crust. Bake 50 to 55 minutes or until top of tart is crusty and deep golden brown and knife inserted in center comes out clean.

Cool completely on wire rack. Cover and store at room temperature until serving time.

Serve It With Style!: Top each serving with a dollop of whipped cream flavored with ground cinnamon, a favorite liqueur and grated orange peel.

White Chocolate Cranberry Tart

Orange Pecan Pie

Makes 8 servings

3 eggs
½ cup GRANDMA'S® Molasses
½ cup light corn syrup
¼ cup orange juice
1 teaspoon grated orange peel
1 teaspoon vanilla
1½ cups whole pecan halves
1 (9-inch) unbaked pie shell
Whipping cream (optional)

Heat oven to 350°F. In large bowl, beat eggs. Add molasses, corn syrup, orange juice, orange peel and vanilla; beat until well blended. Stir in pecans. Pour into unbaked pie shell. Bake 30 to 45 minutes or until filling sets. Cool on wire rack. Serve with whipping cream, if desired.

No Bake Peanut Butter Pie

Makes 1 pie

4 ounces cream cheese
1 cup confectioners' sugar, sifted
1 cup crunchy peanut butter
½ cup milk
8 ounces frozen whipped topping, thawed
1 deep-dish graham cracker or chocolate-flavored crust

In large mixer bowl combine cream cheese and confectioners' sugar; mix well. Add peanut butter and mix. Slowly add milk and mix well. Fold in whipped topping. Pour into pie shell and cover. Freeze for at least 30 minutes. If desired, drizzle each serving with chocolate syrup.

Favorite recipe from *Peanut Advisory Board*

Orange Pecan Pie

simple breads

Pumpkin Bread

Makes 2 loaves

1 package (about 18 ounces) yellow cake mix
1 can (16 ounces) solid pack pumpkin
⅓ cup GRANDMA'S® Molasses
4 eggs
1 teaspoon cinnamon
1 teaspoon nutmeg
⅓ cup nuts, chopped (optional)
⅓ cup raisins (optional)

Preheat oven to 350°F. Grease two 9×5-inch loaf pans.

Combine all ingredients in a large bowl and mix well. Beat at medium speed 2 minutes. Pour into prepared pans. Bake 60 minutes or until toothpick inserted into center comes out clean.

Hint: Serve with cream cheese or preserves, or top with cream cheese frosting or ice cream.

Pumpkin Bread

Cranberry Cheesecake Muffins

Makes 12 muffins

Prep and Bake Time: 30 minutes

> **1 package (3 ounces) cream cheese, softened**
> **4 tablespoons sugar, divided**
> **1 cup reduced-fat (2%) milk**
> **⅓ cup vegetable oil**
> **1 egg**
> **1 package (about 15 ounces) cranberry quick bread mix**

Preheat oven to 400°F. Grease 12 muffin cups.

Beat cream cheese and 2 tablespoons sugar in small bowl until well blended.

Beat milk, oil and egg in large bowl until blended. Stir in quick bread mix just until dry ingredients are moistened.

Fill muffin cups ¼ full with batter. Drop 1 teaspoon cream cheese mixture into center of each cup. Spoon remaining batter over cream cheese mixture.

Sprinkle batter with remaining 2 tablespoons sugar. Bake 17 to 22 minutes or until golden brown. Cool 5 minutes. Remove from muffin cups to wire rack to cool.

Cranberry Cheesecake Muffins

Gooey Caramel and Chocolate Pecan Rolls

Makes 24 rolls

> **2 loaves (1 pound each) frozen white bread dough**
> **1 jar (12 ounces) caramel ice cream topping**
> **⅔ cup coarsely chopped pecans**
> **1 cup semisweet chocolate chips, divided**
> **4 tablespoons butter, divided**

1. Thaw bread dough according to package directions.

2. Preheat oven to 375°F. Divide caramel topping evenly between two 9-inch round cake pans; spread in thin layer. Sprinkle pecans evenly over caramel.

3. Microwave ⅔ cup chocolate chips and 2 tablespoons butter in medium microwavable bowl on HIGH (100% power) for 30 seconds; stir. Microwave for 20 second intervals, if necessary, stirring until smooth; set aside.

4. On lightly floured surface, roll one loaf bread dough into 12×8-inch rectangle. Spread half chocolate mixture over dough. Beginning from the long side, roll up jelly-roll style to form 12-inch log, pinching seam to seal. Slice into 12 rolls; arrange cut side down in 1 prepared pan. Repeat with remaining dough and chocolate mixture.

5. Cover; let rise in warm place until nearly doubled, about 1 hour. Uncover; bake 20 to 25 minutes. Immediately invert onto serving plates.

6. Melt remaining ⅓ cup chocolate chips and 2 tablespoons butter in microwave as directed in step 3. Drizzle over warm rolls.

Gooey Caramel and Chocolate Pecan Rolls

Streusel Coffeecake

Makes 24 servings

Preparation Time: 25 minutes
Cook Time: 40 minutes
Cooling Time: 2 hours
Total Time: 3 hours and 5 minutes

> 32 **CHIPS AHOY!**® **Chocolate Chip Cookies, divided**
> 1 **(18- to 18½-ounce) package yellow or white cake mix**
> ½ cup **BREAKSTONE'S**® **or KNUDSEN**® **Sour Cream**
> ½ cup **PLANTERS**® **Pecans, chopped**
> ½ cup **BAKER'S**® **ANGEL FLAKE**® **Coconut**
> ¼ cup **packed brown sugar**
> 1 **teaspoon ground cinnamon**
> ⅓ cup **margarine or butter, melted**
> **Powdered sugar glaze (optional)**

1. Coarsely chop 20 cookies; finely crush remaining 12 cookies. Set aside.

2. Prepare cake mix batter according to package directions; blend in sour cream. Stir in chopped cookies. Pour batter into greased and floured 13×9×2-inch baking pan.

3. Mix cookie crumbs, pecans, coconut, brown sugar and cinnamon; stir in margarine or butter. Sprinkle over cake batter.

4. Bake at 350°F for 40 minutes or until toothpick inserted in center of cake comes out clean. Cool completely. Drizzle with powdered sugar glaze if desired. Cut into squares to serve.

Streusel Coffeecake

Cinnamon Chip Filled Crescents

Makes 16 crescents

> **2 cans (8 ounces each) refrigerated quick crescent dinner rolls**
> **2 tablespoons butter or margarine, melted**
> **1⅔ cups (10-ounce package) HERSHEY'S Cinnamon Chips, divided**
> **Cinnamon Chips Drizzle (recipe follows)**

Heat oven to 375°F. Unroll dough; separate into 16 triangles.

Spread melted butter on each triangle. Sprinkle 1 cup cinnamon chips evenly over triangles; gently press chips into dough. Roll from shortest side of triangle to opposite point. Place, point side down, on ungreased cookie sheet; curve into crescent shape.

Bake 8 to 10 minutes or until golden brown. Drizzle with Cinnamon Drizzle. Serve warm.

Cinnamon Chips Drizzle: Place remaining ⅔ cup chips and 1½ teaspoons shortening (do not use butter, margarine, spread or oil) in small microwave-safe bowl. Microwave at HIGH (100%) 1 minute; stir until chips are melted.

Cinnamon Chip Filled Crescents

Orange Cinnamon Swirl Bread

Makes 1 loaf (12 slices)

BREAD

1 package DUNCAN HINES® Bakery-Style Cinnamon Swirl Muffin Mix

1 egg

⅔ cup orange juice

1 tablespoon grated orange peel

ORANGE GLAZE

½ cup confectioners' sugar

2 to 3 teaspoons orange juice

1 teaspoon grated orange peel

Quartered orange slices, for garnish (optional)

1. Preheat oven to 350°F. Grease and flour 8½×4½×2½-inch loaf pan.

2. For bread, combine muffin mix and contents of topping packet from mix in large bowl. Break up any lumps. Add egg, ⅔ cup orange juice and 1 tablespoon orange peel. Stir until moistened, about 50 strokes. Knead swirl packet from mix for 10 seconds before opening. Squeeze contents on top of batter. Swirl into batter with knife or spatula, folding from bottom of bowl to get an even swirl. *Do not completely mix in.* Pour into pan. Bake at 350°F 55 to 60 minutes or until toothpick inserted in center comes out clean. Cool in pan 10 minutes. Loosen loaf from pan. Invert onto cooling rack. Turn right side up. Cool completely.

3. For orange glaze, place confectioners' sugar in small bowl. Add orange juice, 1 teaspoon at a time, stirring until smooth and desired consistency. Stir in 1 teaspoon orange peel. Drizzle over loaf. Garnish with orange slices, if desired.

Tip: If glaze becomes too thin, add more confectioners' sugar. If glaze is too thick, add more orange juice.

Orange Cinnamon Swirl Bread

Fast Pesto Focaccia

Makes 16 squares

Prep and Cook Time: 20 minutes

> **1 can (10 ounces) pizza crust dough**
> **2 tablespoons prepared pesto**
> **4 sun-dried tomatoes packed in oil, drained**

Preheat oven to 425°F. Lightly grease 8×8×2-inch pan. Unroll pizza dough; fold in half and pat into pan.

Spread pesto evenly over dough. Chop tomatoes or snip with kitchen scissors; sprinkle over pesto. Press tomatoes into dough. Make indentations in dough every 2 inches using wooden spoon handle.

Bake 10 to 12 minutes or until golden brown. Cut into squares and serve warm or at room temperature.

Quick Corn Bread with Chilies 'n' Cheese

Makes 16 servings

> **1 package (12 to 16 ounces) corn bread or corn muffin mix**
> **1 cup (4 ounces) shredded Monterey Jack cheese, divided**
> **1 can (4 ounces) chopped green chilies, drained**
> **1 envelope LIPTON® RECIPE SECRETS® Vegetable Soup Mix**

Prepare corn bread mix according to package directions; stir in ½ cup cheese, chilies and vegetable soup mix. Pour batter into lightly greased 8-inch baking pan; bake as directed. While warm, top with remaining ½ cup cheese. Cool completely on wire rack. To serve, cut into squares.

Fast Pesto Focaccia

acknowledgments

The publisher would like to thank the companies and organizations listed below for the use of their recipes and photographs in this publication.

CHIPS AHOY!® Chocolate Chip Cookies

Duncan Hines® and Moist Deluxe® are registered trademarks of Aurora Foods Inc.

Eagle® Brand

Grandma's® is a registered trademark of Mott's, Inc.

Hershey Foods Corporation

Keebler® Company

Kraft Foods Holdings

© Mars, Incorporated 2002

Peanut Advisory Board

The Quaker® Oatmeal Kitchens

The J.M. Smucker Co.

Unilever Bestfoods North America

index

Apple-Raisin Cobbler Pie, 34

Banana Split Cupcakes, 30

Caramel-Pecan Pie, 42
Chips Ahoy!® Wiches, 8
Chocolate Chip 'n Oatmeal Cookies, 12
Chocolate Macadamia Chippers, 14
Chocolate Nut Bars, 16
Chocolate Peanut Butter Chip Cookies, 14
Chocolate Peanut Butter Pie, 42
Chocolate Toffee Crunch Fantasy, 28
Cinnamon Chip Filled Crescents, 56
Cinnamon Chips Drizzle, 56
Coconut Clouds, 10
Coconut Raspberry Bars, 20
Confetti Pie, 36
Cranberry Cheesecake Muffins, 50
Creamy Lemon Bars, 22
Crispy's Irresistible Peanut Butter Marbles, 4

Decadent Brownie Pie, 40

Easy Cappuccino Cake, 24
Easy Egg Nog Pound Cake, 32

Easy Lemon Cookies, 12
Easy Turtle Squares, 18

Fast Pesto Focaccia, 60
Flourless Peanut Butter Cookies, 10

Gooey Caramel and Chocolate Pecan Rolls, 52

Luscious Lemon Poke Cake, 26

No Bake Peanut Butter Pie, 46
Nutty Lemon Crescents, 6

Orange Cinnamon Swirl Bread, 58
Orange Pecan Cookies, 8
Orange Pecan Pie, 46

Peanut Butter Chipwiches, 8
Pumpkin Bread, 48
Pumpkin Pie Crunch, 38

Quick Corn Bread with Chilies 'n' Cheese, 60

Streusel Coffeecake, 54

3-Minute No-Bake Cookies, 6

White Chocolate Cranberry Tart, 44

METRIC CONVERSION CHART

VOLUME MEASUREMENTS (dry)

1/8 teaspoon = 0.5 mL
1/4 teaspoon = 1 mL
1/2 teaspoon = 2 mL
3/4 teaspoon = 4 mL
1 teaspoon = 5 mL
1 tablespoon = 15 mL
2 tablespoons = 30 mL
1/4 cup = 60 mL
1/3 cup = 75 mL
1/2 cup = 125 mL
2/3 cup = 150 mL
3/4 cup = 175 mL
1 cup = 250 mL
2 cups = 1 pint = 500 mL
3 cups = 750 mL
4 cups = 1 quart = 1 L

VOLUME MEASUREMENTS (fluid)

1 fluid ounce (2 tablespoons) = 30 mL
4 fluid ounces (1/2 cup) = 125 mL
8 fluid ounces (1 cup) = 250 mL
12 fluid ounces (1 1/2 cups) = 375 mL
16 fluid ounces (2 cups) = 500 mL

WEIGHTS (mass)

1/2 ounce = 15 g
1 ounce = 30 g
3 ounces = 90 g
4 ounces = 120 g
8 ounces = 225 g
10 ounces = 285 g
12 ounces = 360 g
16 ounces = 1 pound = 450 g

DIMENSIONS

1/16 inch = 2 mm
1/8 inch = 3 mm
1/4 inch = 6 mm
1/2 inch = 1.5 cm
3/4 inch = 2 cm
1 inch = 2.5 cm

OVEN TEMPERATURES

250°F = 120°C
275°F = 140°C
300°F = 150°C
325°F = 160°C
350°F = 180°C
375°F = 190°C
400°F = 200°C
425°F = 220°C
450°F = 230°C

BAKING PAN SIZES

Utensil	Size in Inches/Quarts	Metric Volume	Size in Centimeters
Baking or Cake Pan (square or rectangular)	8×8×2	2 L	20×20×5
	9×9×2	2.5 L	23×23×5
	12×8×2	3 L	30×20×5
	13×9×2	3.5 L	33×23×5
Loaf Pan	8×4×3	1.5 L	20×10×7
	9×5×3	2 L	23×13×7
Round Layer Cake Pan	8×1½	1.2 L	20×4
	9×1½	1.5 L	23×4
Pie Plate	8×1¼	750 mL	20×3
	9×1¼	1 L	23×3
Baking Dish or Casserole	1 quart	1 L	—
	1½ quart	1.5 L	—
	2 quart	2 L	—